Ovis
Has Trouble with Eating

written by Kelly Beins   illustrated by Christine Tueeille Merry

BLUE MUSTANG PRESS

Blue Mustang Press
Boston, Massachusetts

First printing

ISBN 978-1-935199-26-7
PUBLISHED BY BLUE MUSTANG PRESS
www.BlueMustangPress.com
Boston, Massachusetts

Ovis
Has Trouble with Eating

written by Kelly Beins   Illustrated by Christine Tuccille Merry

www.ovisthesheep.com

Ovis
Has Trouble with Eating

written by Kelly Beins   Illustrated by Christine Tuccille Merry

Dear Reader,

1 in 15 school-aged children experiences sensory differences, and children with sensory challenges often struggle with eating. There is currently no medical diagnosis of sensory processing disorder, but research and the knowledge base around picky eating is now showing that "avoidant eating" is a real thing (Cano et. al, 2015; Daniel et. al, 2008; Schwartz, 2000).

Parenting a child with sensory differences can be stressful, and parenting a child who won't eat, with or without a diagnosis, can take stress to a whole new level! The challenges of trying to parent a picky eater arise daily because eating is an essential part of life that happens (or is supposed to happen) multiple times a day. But contrary to what many people believe, some children truly won't eat when they are hungry, and they need outside support to learn, or relearn, eating skills. Many parents need outside support, such as occupational therapy, to learn unique ways of helping their reluctant eater, and to change dynamics that have arisen over many stressful years of trying numerous ways to feed their children.

We hope Ovis can be part of that initial support. There are many ways to support a picky eater and varied types of programs, including occupational therapy (OT). This Ovis story is not intended to replace formal intervention, but it introduces some first-line strategies consistent with the "SOS Approach to Eating" (Toomey & Ross, 2011), and we hope it helps you and your child, student, client, or friend in reducing the stress they feel regarding eating. As in our first Ovis book, "Ovis Has Trouble with School," we hope you can find in Ovis, and in his family, a character to whom you can relate. We also hope this book (and others to come) helps to raise awareness and build connections around some of the common but challenging experiences faced by those living with sensory processing disorder.

Sensation is a human experience and by reading to children we support various sensory systems and create a nurturing and welcoming place for them to feel connected, both to themselves and to other people. This alone is a good place to start when trying to support a child with sensory processing differences.

I look forward to sharing more stories of Ovis and hope you will continue to share with me, your stories of Ovis in your life!

Kelly Beins
Occupational Therapist (and sensory mom)

Ovis doesn't like to eat.

He thinks eating is B-A-A-D!

Ovis chews his wool. He chews the buttons on his jacket. He even chews his pencil.

But Ovis HATES to chew
his clover or any of his
food at mealtime.
He especially hates grass stew.

"Please eat!" begs Mrs. Ovis.

"Your body needs food!" insists Mr. Ovis.

Ovis cries, "It's B-A-A-D!"

He thinks it feels weird, smells bad, and tastes gross.
But everyone else eats their sheep food.
Why can't he?

So Mrs. Ovis bought a new kind of clover.

Ovis wouldn't eat. But he drank a LOT of clover milk.

Mrs. Ovis made alfalfa soup so Ovis wouldn't have to chew it. Ovis wouldn't eat.

But he filled his bowl
with crackers until it overflowed.

And she made forbes popsicles, clover smoothies, boiled, steamed, and shredded grass, hay noodles with grass seed sauce, and strawberry and alfalfa-butter sandwiches—all in one meal!

But Ovis STILL WOULDN'T EAT.

One day during lunch at sheep school, Mrs. Sheep Dog, the OT*, noticed that Ovis wasn't eating.

Poor Ovis, thought Mrs. Sheep dog. He looks miserable.

*Pediatric Occupational Therapists (OTs) use scientific evidence about how the brain and body work to help children and families participate in daily activities (occupations) they need or want to do.

Poor Mr. and Mrs. Ovis.
They WERE miserable!

The next week at sheep school...

"Try this." said Mrs. Sheep dog, as she made a train using the clover cookies Mrs. Ovis had packed in Ovis' lunch. Ovis watched…but he didn't eat, even though he used to love those cookies.

The next day at sheep school...

"Try this." said Mrs. Sheep dog, as she gave Ovis his heavy blanket, a special green placemat, and made a picture using grass seed sauce on Ovis' plate. Hmmm…wondered Ovis…he loved green, so he made a picture and smelled it, but he still didn't eat.

On Friday before lunch, Mrs. Sheep dog invited Ovis into the pasture to play. But not to eat.

They just had fun with the food and laughed.

Mrs. Sheep dog called Mr. and Mrs. Ovis to talk on the phone and share some ideas. Back at home, Ovis sat with his heavy blanket and new placemat, and on his plate was...

one   piece   of   grass.

Ovis looked at the grass and remembered the fun he had. Then...he tried it, carefully, only a lick, while no one was looking...

Ovis' parents wanted to jump for joy! They wanted to cheer and clap. They wanted to hug him and squeeze him and say,

"Yay Ovis! You tried it!"

But they didn't.

Mrs. Ovis asked,

Ovis, How was school?

Mr. Ovis said,

Knock Knock... who's there? Green... Your favorite color!

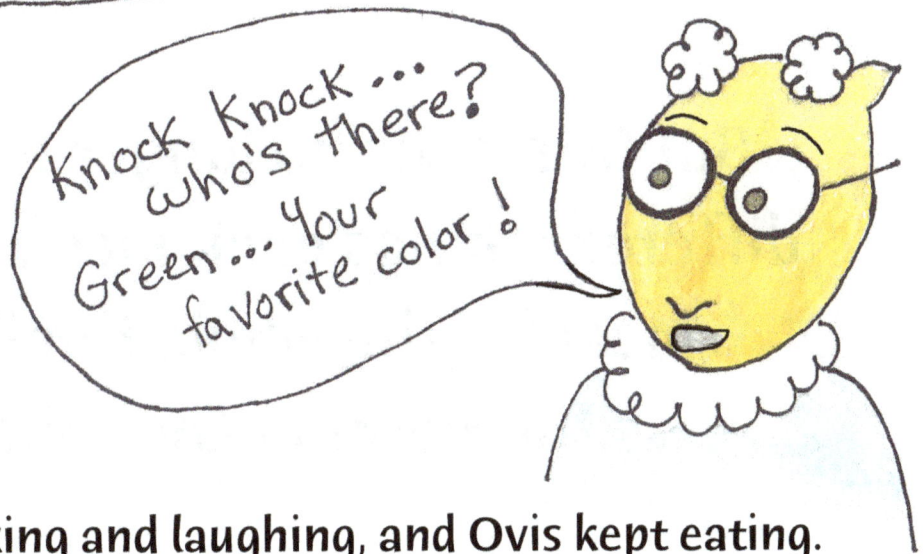

They kept talking and laughing, and Ovis kept eating.

Ovis sees the OT outside of sheep school every week. They call it food school. Now, Ovis helps to cook dinner. And every time Ovis sits down to eat, Mr. and Mrs. Ovis make sure Ovis has his placemat and blanket and a food they know he will eat.

But Mrs. Ovis no longer makes five different things each meal; she makes ONE meal for the whole family, including something Ovis likes.

Sometimes Ovis only eats his favorites, and that's o.k. for now. Mr. Ovis tells a new joke at the table every night. Ovis has fun with his family instead of worrying while he eats.

And now, after trying his
sheep food

over

and over

and over,

Ovis does eat a few
leaves most meals.

He eats different
food shapes and
he's learned he
really likes
strawberry and
alfalfa butter
sandwiches.

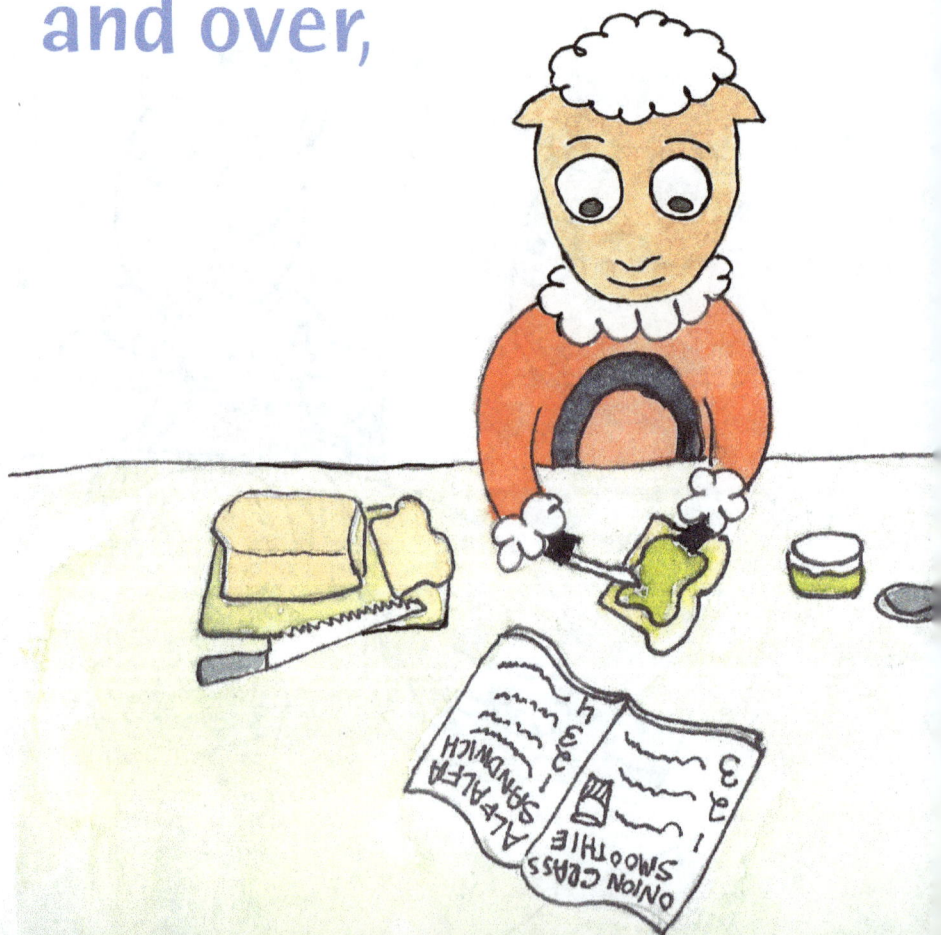

Ovis still doesn't eat very much and he still hates grass stew, but now when Ovis doesn't like a food, he and his parents know what to do.

Ovis is learning that although eating may not always be G-R-E-A-A-T

It's also not so B-A-A-D after all!

www.ingramcontent.com/pod-product-compliance
Lightning Source LLC
LaVergne TN
LVHW061342060426
835511LV00014B/2067